VARIOUS RETURNS

VARIOUS RETURNS

JOAN DOWNAR

A SELECTION OF POSTHUMOUS POEMS

Edited By Michael Payne

Shoestring Press

All rights reserved. No part of this work covered by the copyright hereon may be reproduced or used in any means – graphic, electronic, or mechanical, including copying, recording, taping, or information storage and retrieval systems – without written permission of the publisher.

Printed by imprintdigital
Upton Pyne, Exeter
www.imprintdigital.net

Typeset by narrator
www.narrator.me.uk
info@narrator.me.uk
033 022 300 39

Published by Shoestring Press
19 Devonshire Avenue, Beeston, Nottingham, NG9 1BS
(0115) 925 1827
www.shoestringpress.co.uk

First published 2014
© Copyright: Joan Downar

The moral right of the author has been asserted.

ISBN 978 1 910323 02 1

JOAN DOWNAR

Joan Downar was born in Highgate, London N6. She sometimes claimed to be a cockney which may not have been true, yet her voice had an attractive echo of Bow Bells within it.

She had one sister, Valerie, who predeceased her by only a year, an event which deeply troubled Joan. It might have been a cruel premonition of her own death which came too soon afterwards. Her father was a policeman of whom she was deeply fond. After he died her mother remarried, but Joan was never happy with her step-father.

I met her at Nottingham Theatre Club, where at first I thought her rather daunting, but soon discovered how wrong this was. We wrote and performed together a series of entertainments which were always a pleasure and I was fortunate to have her as a close friend for nearly forty years.

Joan could be described as 'elegant', a term sometimes used for a woman slightly above average in stature. As a child she had been self-conscious about her size, so that in her younger days she had dressed severely. However, after her marriage to Albert Appleton, she gained confidence and her wardrobe became very stylish. She had a beautiful speaking voice and to hear her read her poems was a privilege few would forget. Although she often broadcast on local radio, sadly there seems to be only one recording still in existence. This is her reading of 'War Jaw', (p. 64).

She began work as a librarian in Deptford, then in 1956 after training as an English teacher, she moved to Nottingham. Joan described herself as a compulsive scribbler of poetry. From 1976 onwards she won many prizes in national competitions. Her work appeared in such varied publications as *Encounter*, *New Statesman*, *Poetry Review* and *The Countryman*.

Her first major collection of poems *The Empire of Light* was published by Peterloo Poets in 1984. This was followed by *The Old Noise of Truth* in 1989. Shortly before her death in 1996 she suggested that she had another collection ready, but left no indication of her intentions. This selection is an attempt to try and fulfil that wish from the scores of unpublished poems she left.

Michael Payne, 2014

CONTENTS

Childhood   1
    Nursery Rhyme   3
    Great Grandmother   4
    Christmas Eve   5
    The Eye I Eyed   6
    Mother's Return   7
    Kay   8

Country Living   9
    Message   11
    Dear Violet   12
    Burning the Stubble   13
    Bonfire   14
    A House Inhabited   15
    Old Farmer   16
    Convolvulus   17
    Tea in the Garden   18
    A Mighty Small Wind   19
    Surfaces   20
    In the Cage   21

Married Life   23
    Black and White   25
    Epiphany   26
    House under Water   27
    The Wedding Party   28
    Summer Fruit   29
    Last Fruits   30

Illness — 31

- A Ghazal for A — 33
- Listening — 34
- Night Tide — 35
- From the Bed — 36
- What's Left — 37
- A History of China — 38

Mourning — 39

- Ashes — 41
- The Letter — 42
- Leaves — 43
- Song at the Gate — 44
- Waiting to Sing — 45
- Sunday Morning — 46
- Through Glass — 47
- Darling Oasis — 48

Afterwards — 49

- Last Comfort — 51
- Second Coming — 52
- Late Love — 53
- An Afternoon — 54

Occasional Pieces — 57

- Tide Mark — 59
- Nativity — 60
- Idyll at Tribschen — 61
- To the Pompeians — 62
- Gavrilo Princip in Sarajevo — 63
- War Jaw — 64
- Untitled: The mound has softened… — 65
- Various Returns — 66

Childhood

In 1939 at the outbreak of war, Joan Downar and her sister Valerie were evacuated from London. They were sent to Wiltshire where inexplicably they were were separated and for Joan's sister this was an unhappy experience, for she disliked the people she was billeted upon. Joan was more fortunate and formed a lifelong attachment to the Pye family she lived with, keeping in touch with their daughter Mary until she died.

Several poems that she wrote about her first experience of country life are to be found in her published collections. Most of these six pieces, however, seem to be about the earlier part of her life.

NURSERY RHYME

What are you afraid of, child?
Oh, the outside world at night,
what lies beneath the earth, the wild
wood, and what's beyond the light,

the horned head, the curved blade,
the cross, the crescent, green man,
tiger and the witches' trade,
the cough, the rash, the bogey's clan,

the changeling, gypsy, Boney, Hun,
the cloudy mushroom. Red, the flight
of metal, fire and gun,
whatever comes to cap the light.

GREAT GRANDMOTHER

When I was a girl we saw the sea
just once a year. The beach I paddled on
had thousands of tiny stones, so pink and cool.
We had a boat; the water was cross-hatched

until it swelled, and then my stomach was strong.
My husband? I forget, but not my fool.
The children, five of them, I closely watched
until they fled. Do you see this picture of me

in white for communion? Church is gone they say –
a museum now – I carry my age about
like a curator, only a few of my gems
preserved. My children's children post

me photographs, those twelve or so stout
strangers and their children – how many of them?
My duty's done. I think of my father, the host
of pebbles, the boat. Their names? I forget to-day.

CHRISTMAS EVE

Christmas Eve, and grandmother says,
'To-night you may take a candle to make
you sleep'. For this is the night of the ancient's visit
whose gifts are only for children and must be left in secret.

But unaccustomed light makes a cave
of the high room, the ceiling gapes,
the smoky whips on the flame stroke the guilty
shades, and not a bit of furniture's familiar.

And, 'Please don't come,' she prays, afraid
the giant traveller will force his way
through shadows to abuse her sight; and sleeps,
while gifts assemble, flame's extinguished,
wax grows cold.

THE EYE I EYED

The eye in the mirror
speculates, broods,
isolates, knows me.
I hated that eye:

too many good
things wilted before it;
the glare of contempt
pre-empted failure.

The eye in the mirror
browns warmly,
coddles, smoothes,
looks unsure,
breaks my heart
with absurdity. It
is my mother's eye;
it belongs to me.

MOTHER'S RETURN

A chair, spidery cane
against intense white glare
that burns behind it from the sea.

Then her face, her body's where
was complicated cane. I must
have made her come.

More pale and thin than life
this image of my grief
with its underweb of cane.

I can see through her, almost,
a woman for whose pain
I cannot make amends,

having engendered more.
Silver fishes leap
seaward through the air.

She is not aware
of me in her absorption.
A murmur in my ear;

she's not all there the –
oven's overflowing
with her husband's hair.

KAY

'Red sky at night,' I told the miss
whose eyes reached only the window's glaze.
The morning sun poured through on her bared
flesh but the peculiar hope of the day
couldn't melt the heart's ice
chip or the shoulder's, and I was scared.

Country Living

In 1972, Joan married Albert Appleton, a man sixteen years her senior, with whom she had already lived for some time. In 1979, Albert's son-in-law bought the Grange, an imposing house and grounds in Thrumpton, a small Trent side village in South Nottinghamshire. When he invited Joan and Albert to share part of the house with him and his family, Joan especially was unsure of the offer, but eventually agreed to the proposal.

It proved to be a happy decision. Albert was an enthusiastic gardener and to be put in charge of the extensive garden was a joy for him. Joan, in turn, came to relish country life as perhaps only a former city dweller could.

'Dear Violet' (p. 12) was written after a close friend (a woman priest) had told her how hard it often was to find anything to say about the deceased at a funeral. I read this poem at Joan's funeral.

MESSAGE

The message read –
Don't shut garage door, suspect
a bird is nesting – scribbled
in the shed above a rack of tools.

Perhaps a gardener's hand
or a departed squire,
but faded; it had been there
years. We felt like fools,

leaving the door up for a phantom bird.
All we could see was an invading briar.
We do not kindly allow
imperatives from the past.

until they haunt us, so
the door was closed for two long days
and opened in the morning on a dying swallow.

DEAR VIOLET

'What can I say about her?' They shake
their heads and consider: 'Well,
she liked flowers… and birds.'
And nothing further to reveal
this elderly woman I must bury.

A prisoned swallow cracks
again and again against the Victorian shell
of coloured glass. Five people stride
behind the suffocating smell
of lilies. One whispers to me, 'Very

late on she'd forty pen-friends, black
white. Everywhere.' Where there are angels
posted around the planet's grid,
communicants, unseen, and insubstantial
reaching towards each other's mystery.

BURNING THE STUBBLE

A crimson sun rests on the rim
of the field. The last roll
of straw like an army's pallet

is lifted away. The time has come
to burn the stubble. They spill
petrol and matches. Yellow

flares startle the pigeons, heavy
bellied as planes while troops
of sparrows fly for the woods.

The trickle and hiss of running fire
swifter than weed makes a rare
rabbit leap and by the hedge

the papery scarlet poppies scorch
and seep. The sweating men
idle with satisfaction

watch the dregs of harvest turn
cindery and black
in innocent imitation,

then spitting their fags out climb the high
turrets of tractors and put the plough in.

BONFIRE

The flame catches, positive,
fast as conviction, holds
the cankered branches
until they are glowing fingers,
picks at the guy who folds
over in pain, alive.

You see how it would have been
for Joan and the others, how faith
would have cracked a little with the twigs
before oblivion; how their
stand wouldn't quench the wrath
of powers blazingly seen.

We stare impassive to the good
fire's heart, its gold
and rose that's taken many
a vicarious saint and city;
the sinister explosions of the old
ideas, the incandescent wood.

But later, in the blue
grey dawn, the gritty
ash'll find our grey
ordinary faces who'll remember,
and moving into darkness we
will let the light through.

A HOUSE INHABITED

Builders took the back wall away,
throwing the bricks round an apple tree.

Four tiny rooms, dinky doll-house,
no bathroom and smoke-dark.

They built more rooms; light rushed in
with the new tenants who lit their fires

and settled in parlour and kitchen
before the plasterer had walled them in.

The old lady had moved about once,
slept upstairs, gardened, cooked,

washed modestly – bathrooms meant
more rent – before the children went

and forgot her. Shrunk in one room,
with old apple boughs on the fire,

ashes crept like grey cats,
and she became invisible.

Innocently, the new man
– white-haired already – takes

a spade and digs it deep into
the distressed earth round the apple tree.

OLD FARMER

The fire grumbles in its grate,
fades unwillingly from red to black.
His skin is bruised like storm-cloud,
his plastic valve a reliable grandfather clock.

"I'd like a little dog," he says,
but it's too late for that: dogs
mean walks. His clothes, rough-washed,
hang permanently becalmed about his thwarted legs.

He once drove shires in perfect
patterns, timed his day
with milk, his year with wheat;
hefted hundredweights. Now he doesn't hear what visitors say

about lambs, eggs or neighbours,
is past weeping, peeps
through lashes to see if you are still
there, and forgetting all his old courtesy, sleeps.

His son has opened up the fields,
has sold the hens, the herd.
Progress, which gave him a heart,
has brought the abandonment of his life. It's hard

living too long for comfort.
Like a beast in quick-lime he'll
be disposed of. New hands,
neutral as the sun, will farm his acres well.

CONVOLVULUS

Convolvulus has come again, assertive,
spearing its way over the delicate clematis,
tougher roses, its papery rolls
and big hearts clinging, blowing its musical shapes
with the wind, new cousins coming every morning.

I remember a London garden
in the thirties when convolvulus made
art nouveau of ugly railway spikes until it crept
among the raspberries and was pulled
down by a rougher hand than wind and burnt.

And now, conservationist,
I let convolvulus adorn
the garden, waiving storm, its white-
faced watchfulness, black holes for eyes,
like Hebrew children at a ghetto wall.

TEA IN THE GARDEN

The Earl Grey, golden
in the one fine china cup,
shivers as an intruding breeze
bursts from the perfect sky.

The garden's framed in the vision,
its rose, amber and viridian
a sun-logged Cezanne,
a season's investment.

Labour is elsewhere. It has
no place here in thought
or conversation, an irrelevance
before the achievement.

The heat invites an aristocratic
pause, but clouds come, painting rain
the cold which thin the blood
and thicken the hand pouring tea.

A MIGHTY SMALL WIND

All along the shallow bank,
anchored at the top under hawthorns,
and in tender hollow at the bottom,
thousands of filaments are shimmering,
an undulating silvery tissue, the colour of wind.

In the field heavy-footed horses
of hazel, chestnut and maize lift their heads,
bow and stamp, having an arrogant knowledge
they do not choose to share. And over
the river, geese feeding lay their necks low,
shrugging off its intimate silky skin.

I watch the glittering flow, thinking first
it is like water, then like prayer flags
whipping desperation into the air;
thinking that unlike geese and horses
I cannot feel it close enough, running
human-shaped, a stream of divination.

SURFACES

On the road out, the prehistoric track
above the river which friends say
always frightens them, I think of marshes,
scrub, the common dowdiness
of habitation, the habits of common life,
the expected rituals of a sad ending,
tearing towards the last living creature
who shared the night with me, willing
his life to go on, and pass the oak left
by a farmer when he unthreaded his fields.
It reaches out to the car, and even
in darkness, beguiles with its pattern.

IN THE CAGE

Opening the door of the cage
I hear the nervous 'chit chit chit.'
The hen blackbird is in again.

She flies breast first
against the wire, first to this corner
then the other. Sudden hush;

she shakes alarm notes, scurrying
under the scarlet racemes, the pearl
and black. Thunder troubles the ear.

She finds the way in,
How can she forget the open door is always,
always the way out? Thunder again.

The air is still and moist,
movement is blotted up. I turn
as in sleep, heavy, to hurry her out,

and she flies straight
to the heart of thunder that's free to strip
the fruits of the earth with its glittering beak.

Married Life

From 1979 to 1989, Joan and Albert had a decade of great happiness living at the Grange in Thrumpton. The house was built around 1694, when it had been part of the Byron family estate. Sadly, it had been ruthlessly 'improved' by its previous owner (its top floor removed and the cellars filled) leaving no evidence of its considerable age. Their living room, although not large, was still known in the village as the 'ballroom'. Nevertheless the acre and a half of garden were Albert's joy. He planted over eight hundred roses, and made an avenue of trees (Leaves p. 43) as well as a secret garden for his grand-daughter. Joan especially loved village life, and quickly became part of its activities.

At that time, to visit Joan and Albert was a memorable event. She was a fine cook, turning every meal into a feast, with Albert growing huge amounts of fruit and vegetables. On leaving them, the boot of the visitors' car was always loaded with quantities of garden produce and flowers.

BLACK AND WHITE

In the garden, in the evening,
there is a certain moment
exciting in its uncertainty
when light and dark are balanced.

The pink of rambler roses,
greedy as flesh in daylight,
leach to grey puffballs
poisonously glowing.

The white cling the longest,
asserting presences;
the leaves give up more easily
drawing on what they hide.

And sweet odours, not of sanctity
but inviolable nonetheless,
cheat on scraps of light,
make something good of blackness.

In the garden, in the evening,
arms familiarly entwined,
what we are and what we've done
need no confession.

EPIPHANY

The time for presents is after the tinsel and turkey
when whiny laughter's exhausted and a proper
grave consideration can be given to who gave what.

Like seers reading bones we ponder the choice,
seeing the giver lift and weigh it in just
the same way, measuring liking or love,

tying it with a knot. The message is not
material; the object tells it all and will be
perhaps, disconcerting, imagined harmony

may dissolve. The truer gifts are not so diaphanous
they almost elude us: the crazy données of dreams,
quite without strings; a moment that opens in

on itself to include us; the presence of one
beyond time, not wrapped in gilt
not actually given, but accepted as miracles.

HOUSE UNDER WATER

Although the house is old
and I have heard knocking,
splashing, wooden groans,
I've never thought its once occupants
returned, or indicated unease.

So walking inland from
the sea of sleep, shaking off
last drops in sight of
the clear coast I wasn't prepared
for the sound of bitter human tears.

I think not mine; this place
is warm, with good food
on the table, there is a tenderness.
The tears were terrible. What land
could they have been falling in ?

THE WEDDING PARTY

The brief neat ceremony concluded
between white garlands – how the ladies
had twisted the stems to get a balance –
the company made for the hall, all
the bottles were opened and liquor ran
quickly sparkling in every eye and tongue.
And after the food the speeches; the bride
stood up defying convention, and sense
was ambushed at every sentence
with jokes; then chairs and tables pushed
to the walls, they began an immoderate
stuttering dance.

You might have imagined
the stench of guttering candles, the yap
of little dogs lapping the slops from the floor.
Outside the moonlight's cool response brushed
over waiting wheat where hedgerows once
had followed each step with a shaver of white.

SUMMER FRUIT

Under the leaves, finger the jade green gooseberries,
ping them into a bowl and pick a curd of elderflower
to make an exotic dish. Pile maroon cherries
on to a plate with peaches and nectarines.

Take a seat to the watery blue shade of the chestnuts.
The sun will drizzle like thick cream through the leaves.
Your knees will open, your breasts become soft globes
fallen towards your waist, their points lost.

You will think of distances: the house, the meal, children.
The hard round ball of griefs you carry will rest, hidden
in the cool grass as if (oh love!) it melted at last
and you could believe it didn't exist.

LAST FRUITS

After the vegetable feast comes fruit,
blackberry, apple, pear.
He names them, piling then on the kitchen table
with dust, leaves, twigs:
Conferences, Russet, Grenadier.

And tiny insects fly to the window
dislocated, confused.
Then the wrack of the first frost
halves the garden. He builds
a bonfire in the mist.

Leaves, stalks, tendrils redden,
blacken. He drags huge
prunings, his face peering through leaves
like a sly carving, a warrior, a green man,

as he mouths at me grinning, 'Birnam.'
And for a moment I know
I shall keep this, in some unclear
future, when gifts are scarce,
and everything I have lets go.

Illness

Early in 1989 Joan's husband, Albert, was discovered to have multiple cancer. He had been a man of great strength and vigour and he died the following April aged 75. Joan nursed him at home throughout his final months. During his illness and death she dealt with her anxiety and worry by writing poetry whenever she could.

A GHAZAL FOR A

Woken before the dawn, I was convinced that you
were doomed, your cough emerging from my dream.

What seemed straightforward, curable, became
a terrible shadow, separated from light.

I rehearsed my sorrow, knew the vacancy of loss,
thought of my friends the widows with tenderness.

Repeated you name, endearments, as if my words
would re-order you molecules, reverse a law.

Even saw sparks of future, a changed world,
even as from this moment the world was changed.

The cough rattled again, close to my ear,
and you awoke, saying you're better.

LISTENING

Listening from downstairs to the breathy rasp,
I think of Keats, how Severn must have felt,
sat in another room, pondering the sheer
bad grace of gods to take a poet
still growing beauty and achievement.

Of course the man upstairs is older,
but the affliction's strange, untreatable.
He beats a hand grown whiter, softer,
as the breathing roughens, knowing the scribble
of new growth in the garden's escaped his grasp.

The hollow clack of last year's leaves
accompanies the opening of the door. I know,
and so does he, the cycling verities of earth,
heart-breaking eternity. We're slow
to find some grace in our lament.

NIGHT TIDE

Reaching out to you in the middle of the night
I touch your back; the cotton's soaked and slippery
and hot; all the little channels let
go their structure as if you'd melt,

like sand under a tide, disperse and be
re-formed. I don't know whether you feel
threatened, you sleep so deeply;
whether you drown in a boiling sea,

one you like to watch and stroll beside
but never enter, one you fear.
I could not be nearer, but the hand
I stretch is insubstantial as sand.

FROM THE BED

The garden drowns in green light.
A woman sinks to the bed.
The mouths of creatures sailing past her
open and close. She hears
no message, but emits one long
radiant note that loops her about,
a signal saying she is still
in home waters though clawed
almost to death. Then a shaft,
daffodil bright, drains the stones
to the gem-like opacity
of her own face, and she surfaces,
hears someone talking about new growth.

WHAT'S LEFT

The intruders came again last night.
I heard their steps, the pressed
boards, the door jamb's squeak. I guessed
they'd take the bits of silver, video
tv, microwave, all the most
passable things. I thought they'd go
without the books, my raw squeezed
words. Outside was bright.
Across the grass some broken tiles
shone silver. In the dead
silence I could hear a train two miles
away. They'd gone, but I was not released:
heavy as gold the dangerous host
of possessions in my head.

A HISTORY OF CHINA

At his deathbed she threw cups, a plate,
not in grief then, but despair
slipping to exasperation.
It is not known if he was shocked.
He died quietly, reaching for no hand but his own.

Then came grief, remorse, a total recall
of their married life. She picked up
pieces and put the pattern
properly together, but left the cracks
displayed like the gold ring on her finger.

(Note by the poet: 'A Chinese method of mending ceramics is to leave a rim of gold between the joined parts to show the piece's history'.)

Mourning

After Albert's death, Joan was often obliged to spend time alone in the Grange at Thrumpton which was not always pleasant for her. Yet she refused offers from friends to stay with her. It saddened her that she was not able to maintain the garden as Albert had done so energetically.

Nonetheless she did as best she could and continued to be an enthusiastic member of village life. She sang in the church choir (Waiting to Sing, p. 45), and was president of the local W.I. for the maximum term allowed. She loved all aspects of village life, the W.I., the cricket suppers, the outings, and especially – the gossip.

ASHES

Not a gilded urn, or a porcelain jar,
but a plastic bottle came
with his ashes.

Heavy; grey flakes, black grits,
these were the loving limbs
that I had kissed.

Oh, we are all changed indeed,
not in the same heaven's
superior mansion,

but here where your war of attrition
ended, private Hiroshima,
your ashes spread

under your roses, your shadow burned
on my skin, indelible
for light-years.

THE LETTER

The letter is meant to console:
"You have lived with a sense of mortality
a long time." But yes. Wasn't childhood,
girlhood, drugged with it, a whole

dark brilliance in every bland
day only sharpened dark with love?
And now I've taken the ultimate dose: my death
would be kind, but I lack a brave hand.

So with your withdrawal comes mine.
After the anguish, desire for you will become
controllable habit, and blackness will be tamed,
familiar, comforting and benign.

LEAVES

A walk down his avenue of trees
naming acer, liviodenron, larch,
all grown since April,
his other possessions reduced to relics.

Already there have been changes,
rises and falls, revolutions: these
would have thrilled him. I search
for his authentic scents, the overspill

of a life, and keep our routine
as if that would cancel time, hinge
me back whole with him, tease
my sight, and like this birthday larch

ring myself round and round
with our history, helpless green
life, and though resisting change;
put out more leaves, more leaves.

SONG AT THE GATE

I am near the head of the queue,
my plate offered, a white disc,
and know you are close behind me.
What nourishment to you
this doubtful food? A dark hand kindly

gives me six black seed
or grains burnt from some bleak store.
I smile and turn to you to say
ironically: 'We'll fatten to feed
on these,' but you recede, my love,
each time I look, further and further away.

WAITING TO SING

I open the door on to blackness,
then note a last blood-red glow
from some saintly robe
and grope past the font to a switch.

There are some who refuse to enter
at night, Christians. What do they fear
to surprise if this is a house
of spirits? I wait for the choir,

the yellow bulb deadening
the damp stones, and long for flesh,
the sight of you transparent
even, and think of the thick

mess of my soul turned corporeal
already, its taste on my tongue sweet
as desert water and wish
to confess, my love, my priest.

SUNDAY MORNING

For a moment, as I gather from the drawer
the necessary implements: knives, spoons,
a spatula, the sun slices its blade
clean across the kitchen, cuts
it in half, shaves my bent head,
and I murmur, 'My darling, my darling,'
not knowing which departed love
– there are several now – I name.

So I begin to prepare the food and cook
a Sunday lunch for myself, and gradually
that sharp brilliance moves round
to slaughter another room, and the light softens,
and I feel this present is bearable,
as the bells in the church tower
swing from extremes and rest their weight,
still shivering with song.

THROUGH GLASS

Standing in the kitchen peeling
potatoes I look up and see
to the extreme right of my eye
through wisteria's defeated tangle
you disappearing. It is not night.

It is late afternoon, bright
and blowsy with leaves. The angle
of your body speaks urgency
so I drop my knife and fly
to all the windows and doors feeling

sure excitement. It must be right
to return where you planted trees
and roses, where we lived at peace
for so many years. You've come to defy
death. My arms ache, and my heart.

But you're not to be found in any part
of the house or garden. Eyes deny
sense. It's age that reveals these
visions, and love that provides this –
even in darkness – this light.

DARLING OASIS

It's such a personal thing, love,
despite weddings, which we didn't have.
Shameful to remember the awful clichés:
you like a well of sweet water
in a dried-up desert world,
me a flower among dunes.

Today I read of Chinese academics
who had studied sand. They say
dry grains of equal size moving
together in soft wind emit sounds
like singing and groaning. And I think –
we did both, quietly.

Afterwards

In the last two years of her life, Joan found solace with another much older man. He had lived in Thrumpton all his life where he had been a farmer's labourer and part of his attraction for her were the stories he told of village life in the past. He was twenty years her senior, but she admitted mischievously that she 'enjoyed being adored'.

LAST COMFORT

Helping the old man dress,
because alone he puts two legs
in one half of the trousers, I listen
again to the events that make
me into a casual nurse:
the fall, the loneliness.

Heaving eighteen stone
of wheat, he was once serene
as his own shires, whose strength
moved the land from season
to season; he was guarded with words
even among his own,

and certainly with caresses. His whole
life urged the manifest
of crop and beast; tears
were rain in distant parts.
Now he weeps. I hold
his unfamiliar body to console.

And think this would have been rash on
an earlier occasion, say
some months ago, quite misunderstood.
How swiftly may we find or lose
the mechanics of passion.

SECOND COMING

Afterwards, after we've left the bed
And drunk the tea, you busy yourself
by the sheer ordinary domesticity
of it, when I want to explain
why I leapt out of bed so soon.
And I can't say it. And you can't see
another man's back in the kitchen
facing the dark, and why when I say:
'I'm shaking,' and you reply 'Me too,'
I can't stand behind you
with dramatic words like *adore*
and fold my arms over your heart.

LATE LOVE

It's the words first – *darling*,
dreams, forever, – that lay
a burden, the ear's balance
trembles. Then the gaze,
a bright demand, unlooked-for.

Flattering, and once it could have been shed
like excess weight, but now
it's unexpected light throws
heavier shadows. Alternatives
underline a darker vocabulary.

AN AFTERNOON

My nose is nervous, but the flannelette sheets
smell of talc; he's emptied lavender
over them and the pillows.

The mattress rolls us together like a gigantic
breaker; we struggle in its breathless trough.
He's cleaned his teeth,

taken a bath: *Anything for my darling.*
Clocks tick on the table, on the wall,
as if he's not afraid of time.

Born too late for one war, too old for the next,
bullets are less real to him than raindrops.
Still are; the planet's wars

are a fantasy, like books, like plays
he can't be doing with. This is real;
the village, the street,

the fields, the woods, the animals, the gossip,
and going to bed without clothes, a novelty
he's making the most of.

His skin is tough, his arms determined,
and his bum is rounded and hard,
unlike the old man –

too long without use, until persuasion
stiffens the sinews. When his family call,
loving and kind,

he dwindles to Dad-in-the-corner,
but now he's the merry ploughboy
with an eye for the women.

Occasional Pieces

The first two poems were written when Joan was still a teacher. After taking early retirement, she and Albert frequently travelled abroad (pp. 61 to 63) including a visit to Bayreuth (p. 61) to hear Wagner's *Ring* Cycle.

Joan held many poetry workshops in various parts of the country and she had a devoted following for her writing classes at the Nottingham University Department of Adult Education. Following Albert's death she took over his weekly column which covered amateur drama for the local evening newspaper. In her new role as drama critic she wrote reviews for scores of shows.

Finally, in remembering her, mention must be made of her fine singing voice, her gift for mimicry and in particular, her great sense of humour. Although she could often be scathing when describing people or events, there was no malice in her nature. She was a very sensuous woman enjoying, when she could, the hedonistic aspects of life.

This posthumous collection, I hope, does justice to her memory and her talent.

M.P.

TIDE MARK

It is... Stephen bends
to the completion of a sentence
he first wrote in the primary school
... a fine day... and looks around
the stuffy room with its window closed.

Our Mick... the brother he protects
from bullies... is at Gran's...
the old girl whose garden he digs...
Our dog died... He cried for days,
I suspect, till the tide ran out. Full stop.

Try some more, I encourage him.
His head swims
from side to side as his pen slips
in the sea of words and he crawls up
the dry beach to a cave of silence.

A flood of oaths fills the playground –
oaths richly
nourished him – yet his gentleness
exceeds definition. Words
are fossils in the precipice of his being.

NATIVITY

"I'm only an angel," said the girl
in the harsh daffodil muslin wings
of a fairy, and gaped when the children roared.

Finally, hand on hip, she became
a schoolgirl again, indignant and naked
as Eve, and stammered the unscripted words
to invisible God in the crib
and made an earth-bound exit. They
who have outgrown fairies, know that angels
in any disguise bring serious news
and never apologise.

(Published in New Poetry 2. Arts Council, 1976.)

IDYLL AT TRIBSCHEN

Crammed on the staircase, trying not to make
their boots squeak or the instruments they held
respond too early, those musicians must
have sensed the magic. In the lovers' bed
Cosima, like Titania, lay entranced
by spells, as music greatly held her
to a climax she herself could not describe.

Queen of his villa perched on its grassy lake –
side mound, she loved the vain and arrogant man
(his fancy hat is now encased in glass)
fed his music and his children and
perhaps would never waken to the darker
sources whence the magic came. When children
died, she'd lost him, and was blind.

TO THE POMPEIANS

If ever you thought about such things,
cool in your colonnades, with the cobalt sky
promising certain crops and exploding vines,
I suppose you'd direct your amusedly careless eye
at the fountain of dancing dogs or the solid port,
the patrician's marbles – this with lascivious wink,
becoming a guffaw at mention of the sport
in the Villa of Mysteries – nothing to link
old Pan, anyway, with the mountainous malice above.
No, life was for getting on with, and on,
a job, a family, and if the gods willed it, love.
They took the spirit, but flesh once gone was gone.
No four-minute warnings to practise before the ash
beclouded your blue. The gentle irony warms,
that those who tried to save their lives, or cash,
survive as indestructible sculptured forms.

GAVRILO PRINCIP IN SARAJEVO

The children's game is picking a straw
from a pile without unbalancing all
the rest. The straws we picked in the poll,
we six, spilled more than we'd argued for.

Chance comes in many disguises; you must
keep grabbing, so when the car stopped
through a fumbled direction, at the coffee shop,
I fired. The museum tells the rest:

you've see my mug-shot, terrified and dark.
The assassin knows his importance on the earth
as scavenger, not avenger, but the wrath
takes years to run through, then the work

of building begins again. Plant
your feet in the matrixes they've made
in concrete on the pavement where I stood.
Half crouch and point your thumb. I haunt

half the world's youth, but many deaths
make one hero, the chance
of seeing clear through circumstance
is doubtful as the light between saint and psychopath.

I only know there was a call
to have the bridge named after me, but it was built
centuries ago, and I feel no guilt,
knowing builders outbalance destroyers after all.

WAR JAW

Whose leg is this? Dear chap,
I think it must be mine
and this would be your hand.
An unfortunate mishap
to be thus met, we a small band
from Willoughby Field,
our fine plumes crushed, you
mopping up from Cromwell's line.

Those Costock ploughmen thrust
us willy-nilly deep
outside the church's wall.
Forgive me, but I must
presume this gourd to be your skull.
Or is it mine? I keep
remembering our encounter, and trust
you manage sleep.

They call this place the War Hill
or the Worrill, and it's food
for thought for innocents
whose only battles are the ill
they bear their neighbours. Whence
think you, come these jaw-bones, blood
adhering, shattered still, and disengaged for good?

Note: In the 1880s some bones disinterred from outside Costock church wall were found to be those of men who had apparently been killed in a minor skirmish between royalists and parliamentarians on a nearby hill, still then called the Worrill. The battle of Willoughby Field had occurred nearby in 1648 in which the cavaliers were crushed by Colonel Rossiter. Joan was asked in 1992 to write a poem commemorating the 250th anniversary of the outbreak of the Civil War.

Untitled: THE MOUND HAS SOFTENED…

The mound has softened in wind and rain,
like vowels over time, and lost its ditch
almost, their makers unimaginable now.

I wonder at the sort of speech they'd offer,
what I'd give in return, and what raw sound
would mean beginning and end, and if they'd matched

complexities with absolutes and found
simple reflections best. In Shakespeare's land
a hedger and ditcher told the actor playing Hamlet

reflecting on divinity, how he *rough-hewed*
his ends. And other men named dandelions
golden boys, and seed-heads, *chimney-sweepers*.

I think, treading this turf in sun and rain,
if those old ones and I could meet they'd vocalise as clear
as birds a recognised vernacular.

Talking to Maggie Smith about the number of grey heads in the audience for *Talking Heads*, I compare them with a field of dandelion clocks. She says that she's read or been told that the Warwickshire folk name for these was 'chimney sweeps', so that Shakespeare's "golden lads all must / As chimney sweepers come to dust" is thus explained. Alan Bennett, *Untold Stories*, 2005, page 191.

Joan wrote this poem ten years before this anecdote.

VARIOUS RETURNS

Sometimes it's a short visit:
'I'm only popping in for a minute,'
but she never said that,

and not always pleasant;
she unsteady, headlong on the pavement,
me heedless ahead.

Or bitterly rowing about waste,
me, that is, wanting to write –
there was no money in it.

Sometimes it's the gloomy grey
of a station, and miles out of her way
she'll kiss me, briefly, goodbye.

She's stayed longer, on a journey,
she to whom a car was a luxury –
when every car was black, briefly

she drove in one – and tears
at me, snaps all the years
she knew me. I can bear

it now, being apart and having
understood in her last suffering
our inextricable despair and loving.

And we've changed: I've proved
her both right and wrong, am soothed
by my own truth.

She now comes peacefully at night, where
she occupies a cane chair,
and white curtains blow against the sea out there.